NATIONAL JOURNEYS

Houghton Mifflin Harcourt

Program Consultants

Shervaughnna Anderson · Marty Hougen
Carol Jago · Erik Palmer · Shane Templeton
Sheila Valencia · MaryEllen Vogt

Consulting Author · Irene Fountas

Cover illustration by Scott Nash.

Copyright © 2017 by Houghton Mifflin Harcourt Publishing Company

Printed in the U.S.A.

ISBN 978-0-544-87242-4

1 2 3 4 5 6 7 8 9 10   0868   25 24 23 22 21 20 19 18 17 16
4500605300   B C D E F G

Unit 1

2

Unit 2

Unit 3

WORDS TO KNOW

High-Frequency Words

I

Vocabulary Reader

Context Cards

Words to Know

Read Together

▶ Read the word.

▶ Talk about the picture.

I

I have a big family!

Your Turn

Talk About It!

What Makes a Family?

by Pam Muñoz Ryan

Families are different. What is the same about all families? Share ideas with a partner.

See What We Can Do

by Susan Gorman-Howe

illustrated by Sue Dennen

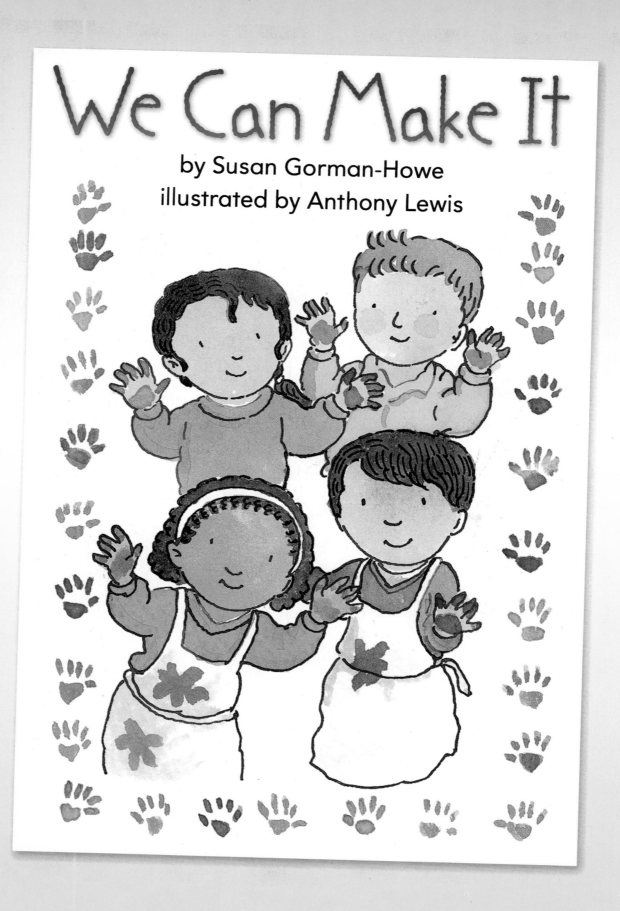

We Can Make It

by Susan Gorman-Howe
illustrated by Anthony Lewis

We Go to School
by Susan Gorman-Howe
illustrated by Maryann Cocca-Leffler

I Like
by Owen Marcus
illustrated by Maribel Suarez

WORDS TO KNOW
High-Frequency Words

like

Vocabulary Reader

At School
by Philip Rush

Context Cards

We like to go to school!

How Do I Use It?
Pam and Jamal like to draw. Do you
like ice cream?

Talk It Over:
Think about things you like. Take turns talking
about them with a partner.

Words to Know

Read Together

▸ Read the word.

▸ Talk about the picture.

like

1

We like to go to school!

Your Turn

Talk About It!

Talk about what happens when the dinosaurs do not follow the rules. Why do we have rules at school?

We Go to School

by Susan Gorman-Howe

illustrated by Maryann Cocca-Leffler

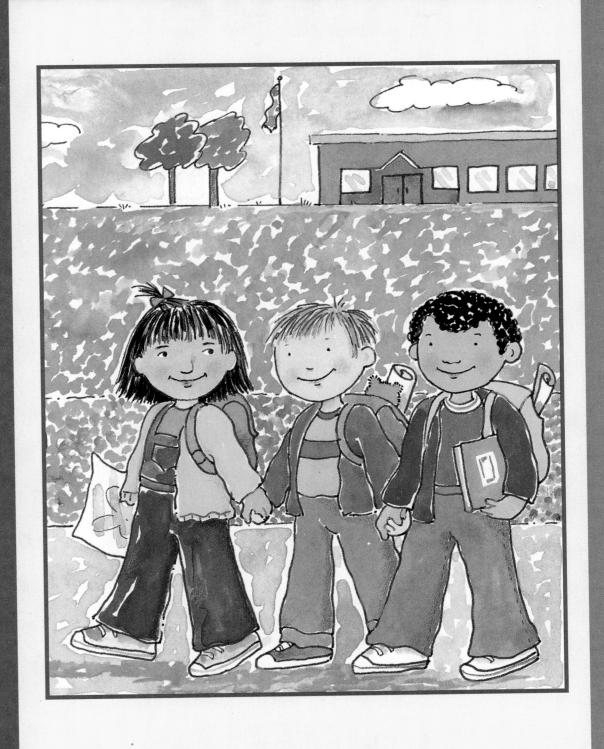

I Like

by Owen Marcus

illustrated by Maribel Suarez

I like .

I like .

I like .

I like .

WORDS TO KNOW
High-Frequency Words

the

Vocabulary Reader

Context Cards

Words to Know

Read Together

► Read the word.

► Talk about the picture.

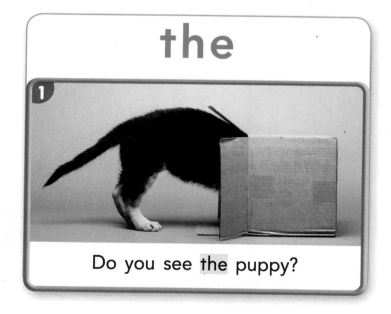

the

1

Do you see the puppy?

Your Turn

Talk About It!

Talk to a friend. Tell why pets need someone to take care of them.

Baby Bear's Family

by Susan Gorman-Howe

illustrated by Angela Jarecki

The Party

by Ron Kingsley

illustrated by Yvette Banek

I like the .

I like the .

I like the ⬤.

I like the .

Mm
by Pat Macnan
illustrated by
Diana Schoenbrun

I Like Mm
by Pat Macnan

WORDS TO KNOW

High-Frequency Words

and

Vocabulary
Reader

Context
Cards

Words to Know

Read Together

▸ Read the word.

▸ Talk about the picture.

and

A worker has a saw **and** a hammer.

Your Turn

Everybody
Works
by Shelley Rotner and Ken Kreisler
Photographs by Shelley Rotner

Talk About It!

What kinds of work do people do? Tell a partner.

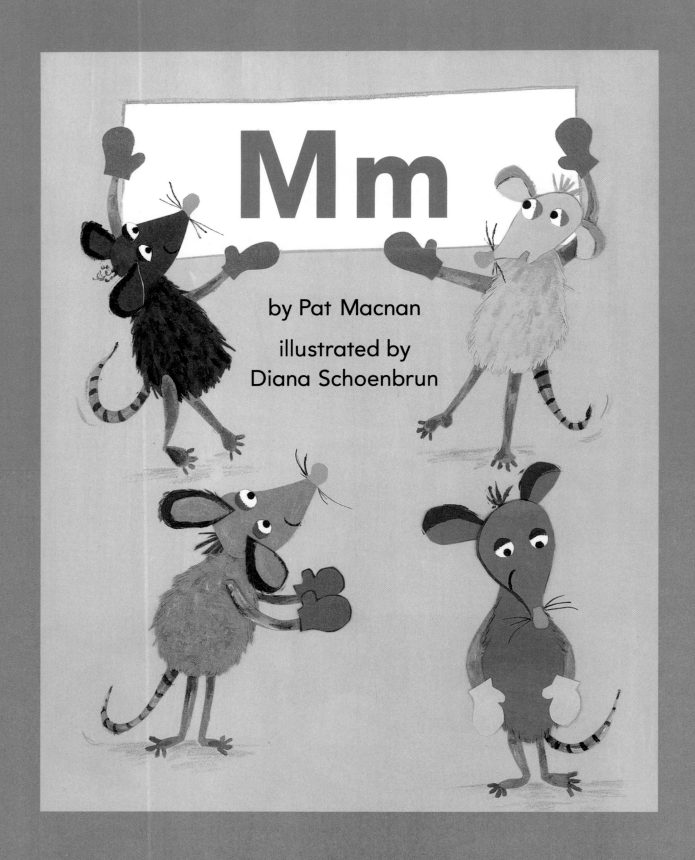

Mm

by Pat Macnan

illustrated by
Diana Schoenbrun

Mm

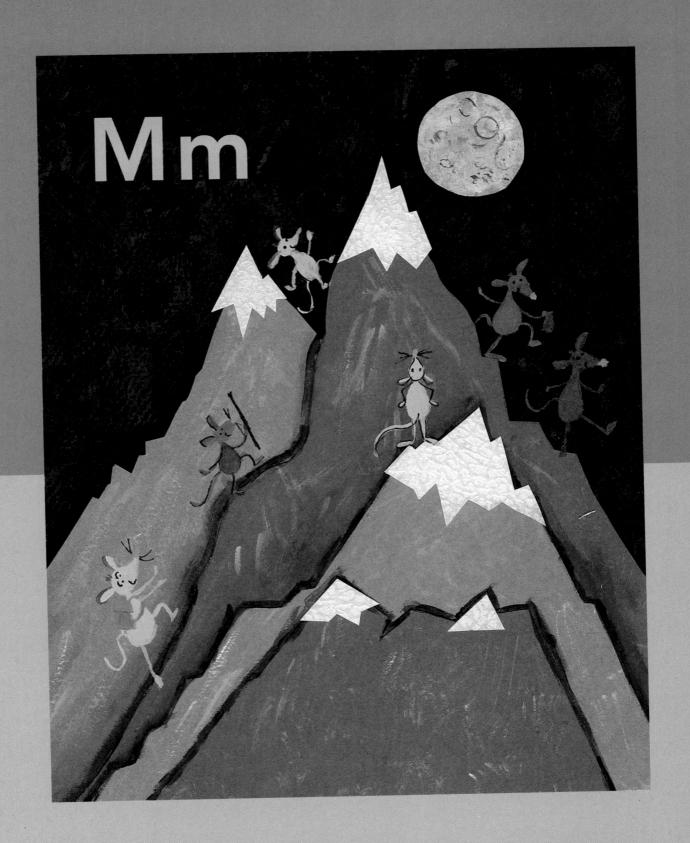

I Like Mm
by Pat Macnan

I like the 🌙.

I like the .

Mm

I like the 🥛.

Mm

I like the ▯ and the ⬡⬡.

Ss
by Pat Macnan
illustrated by Diana Schoenbrun

I Like Ss
by Pablo Lopez

WORDS TO KNOW
High-Frequency Words

I
like

Vocabulary
Reader

Make a Kite
By Becca Houston
HOUGHTON MIFFLIN

Context
Cards

I have a big family!

Words to Know

Read Together

▶ You learned these words. Use each one in a sentence.

I

I have a big family!

like

We like to go to school!

Your Turn

Talk About It!

The Handiest Things in the World
ANDREW CLEMENTS
Photographs by Raquel Jaramillo

How do tools help us do things with our hands?
Tell a partner what you think.

Ss

by Pat Macnan

illustrated by Diana Schoenbrun

51

I Like Ss

by Pablo Lopez

I like the .

Ss

I like the .

Ss

I like the ☀.

I like the 🥤 and the 🥪.

WORDS TO KNOW

High-Frequency Words

see

Vocabulary Reader

Context Cards

Words to Know

Read Together

▸ Read the word.

▸ Talk about the picture.

see

What can you **see** in the city?

Your Turn

Talk About It!

How do you use your senses to learn about the world? Tell a friend.

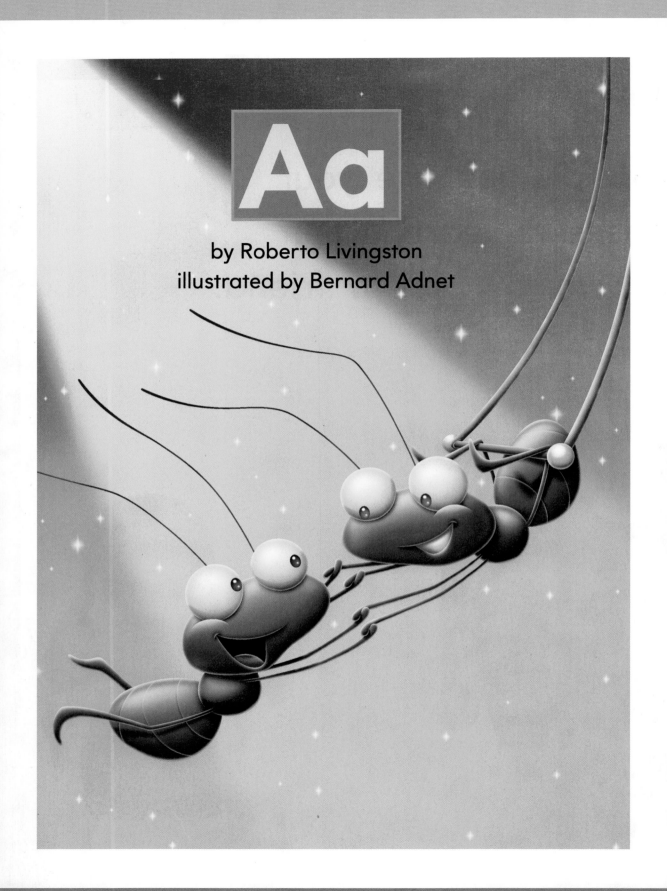

Aa

by Roberto Livingston
illustrated by Bernard Adnet

Aa

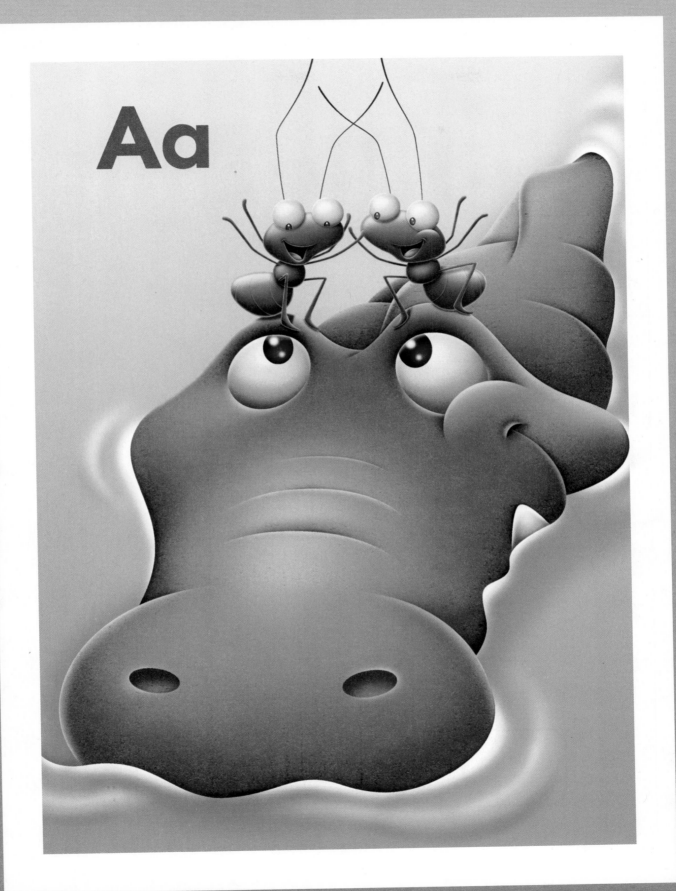

I See

by Sheila Hoffman

I see the .

Aa

I see the .

Aa

I see the .

Aa

I see the .

7

Tt
by Nimesh Sing
illustrated by Priscilla Burris

We Like Toys
by Matthew Lorer

WORDS TO KNOW

High-Frequency Words

we

Vocabulary Reader

Context Cards

Words to Know

Read Together

▸ Read the word.

▸ Talk about the picture.

we

Our cat purrs when **we** pet her.

Your Turn

Talk About It!

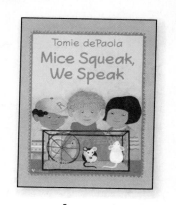

Tomie dePaola
Mice Squeak,
We Speak

How do people and animals communicate? Talk about it with a friend. Use words from the **Big Book** as you share ideas.

Tt

by Nimesh Sing

illustrated by Priscilla Burris

Tt

Tt

We Like Toys

by Matthew Lorer

Tt

I like the .

Tt

We like the .

Tt

We like the .

8

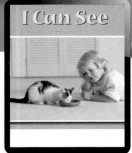

WORDS TO KNOW

High-Frequency Words

a

Vocabulary Reader

Context Cards

Words to Know

▶ Read the word.

▶ Talk about the picture.

a

This rabbit sits on a log.

Your Turn

Talk About It!

Why do different animals move in different ways? Talk about it with a friend.

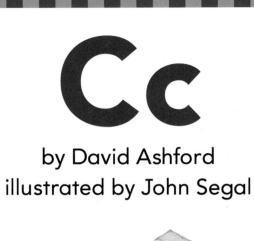

Cc

by David Ashford

illustrated by John Segal

Cc

I Can See

by Laticia Craven

I see a .

Cc

I see a .

I see a .

Cc

I see a .

WORDS TO KNOW

High-Frequency Words

to

Vocabulary Reader

Context Cards

Words to Know

Read Together

▶ Read the word.

▶ Talk about the picture.

to

We like to ride our bikes!

Your Turn

Talk About It!

Why do people use wheels?
Talk with a partner.

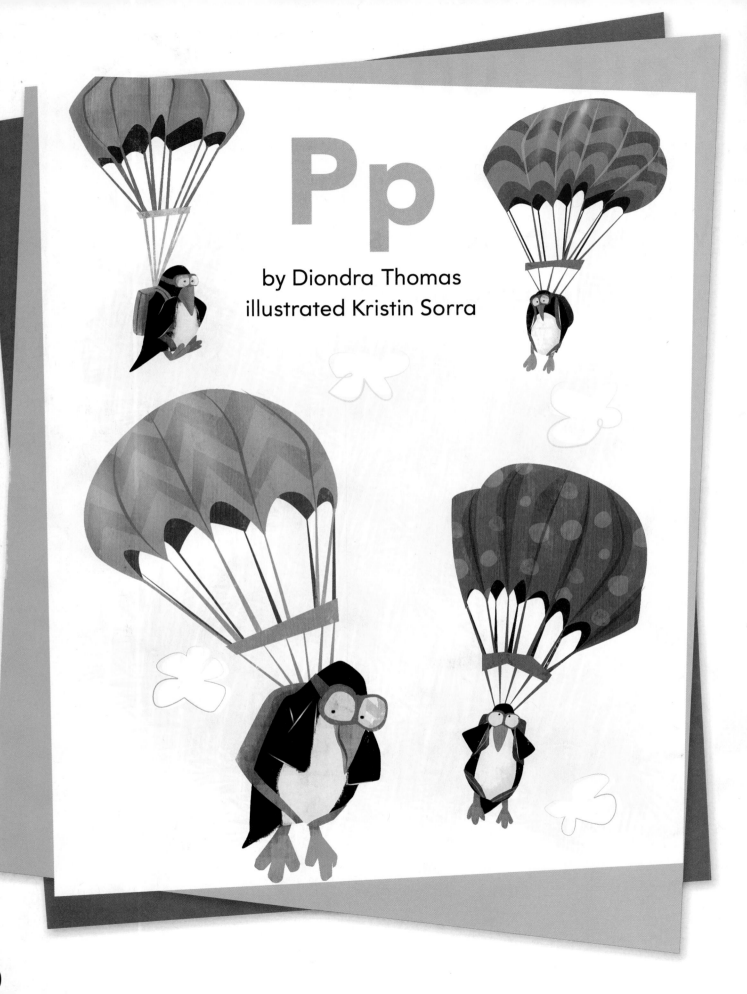

Pp

by Diondra Thomas
illustrated Kristin Sorra

Pp

I Like Animals

by Sydney Mueller

I like to see 🐷🐷 .

Pp

I like to see .

Pp

I like to see 🐻🐻🐻 .

Pp

I like to see 🦜🦜 .

WORDS TO KNOW

High-Frequency Words

see

we

Vocabulary Reader

Context Cards

Words to Know

▸ You learned these words. Use each one in a sentence.

see

What can you **see** in the city?

we

Our cat purrs when **we** pet her.

Your Turn

Talk About It!

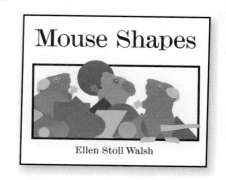

Mouse Shapes

Ellen Stoll Walsh

What do the mice make with shapes in the **Big Book?** What can we create with shapes? Talk with a partner.

Mmmm, Good!

by Angela Ferie
illustrated Ana Ochoa

I see .

I like .

We like .

We like to see .

The Playground

by Paul Falcon

illustrated by Robin Oz

I like the .

I like to .

We see the .

We like the .

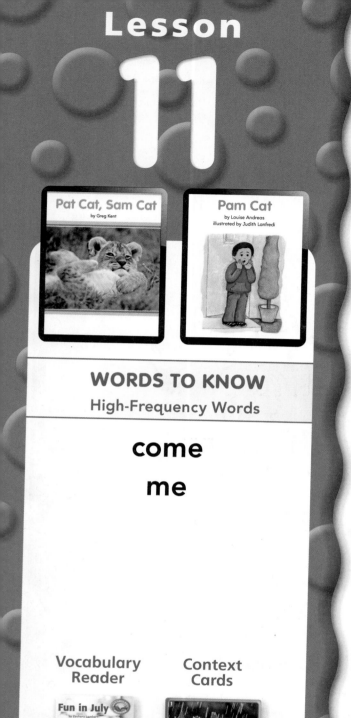

Pat Cat, Sam Cat
by Greg Kent

Pam Cat
by Louise Andreas
illustrated by Judith Lanfredi

WORDS TO KNOW

High-Frequency Words

come

me

Vocabulary
Reader

Context
Cards

Fun in July
by Zachary Lambert

The rain will come down in spring.

Words $\quad$ Read Together

to Know

▶ Read the words.

▶ Talk about the pictures.

come

The rain will **come** down in spring.

me

This hat is for **me**.

Your Turn

Talk About It!

JUMP into JANUARY
A Journey Around the Year
Stella Blackstone
Maria Carluccio

How does the weather change in different months and seasons? Talk to a friend about it.

Pat Cat, Sam Cat

by Greg Kent

Pat Cat, Pat Cat.
I am Pat Cat.

Come to me, Pat Cat!
Pat Cat sat.

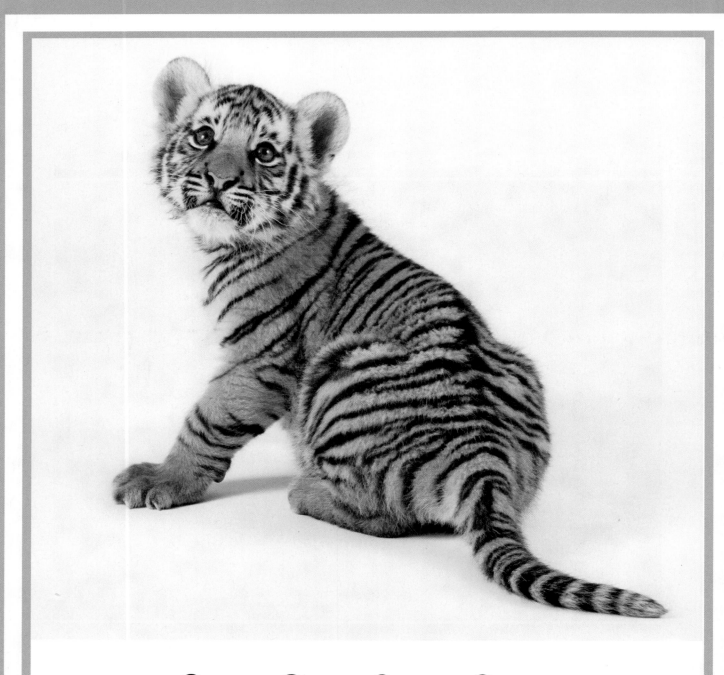

Sam Cat, Sam Cat.
I am Sam Cat.

Come to me, Sam Cat!
Sam Cat sat.

Pam Cat

by Louise Andreas

illustrated by Judith Lanfredi

Pam Cat! Pam Cat! Pam Cat!
Pam Cat! Pam Cat! Pam Cat!

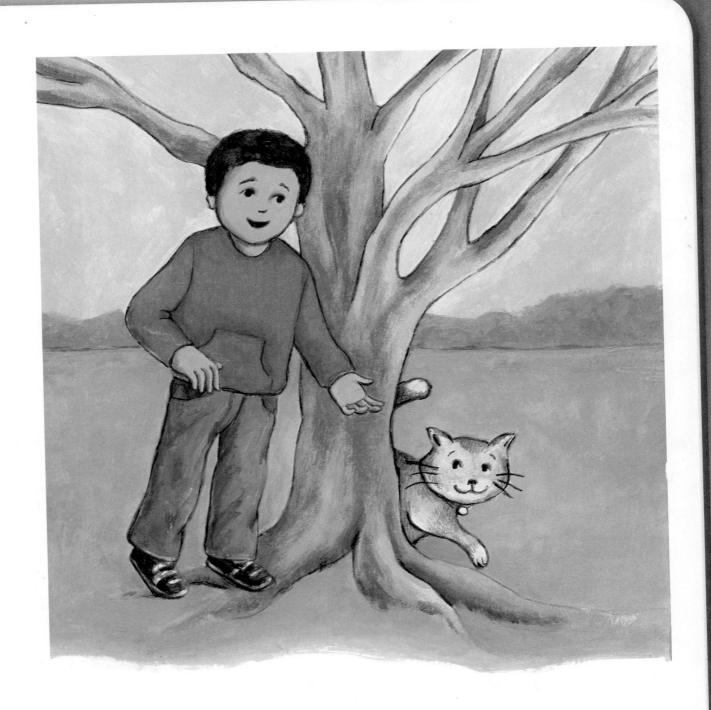

I see Pam Cat.
Come to me, Pam Cat.

Pam Cat sat.
Pam Cat and I sat.

I pat Pam Cat.
I pat and pat Pam Cat.

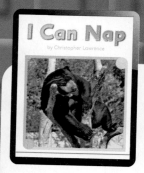

WORDS TO KNOW
High-Frequency Words

with

my

Vocabulary Reader

Context Cards

Words to Know

Read Together

▸ Read the words.

▸ Talk about the pictures.

with

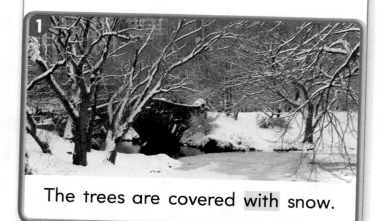

The trees are covered **with** snow.

my

The snowman wears **my** scarf.

Your Turn

Talk About It!

What do animals do when the weather changes? Talk to a partner about it.

I Can Nap

by Christopher Lawrence

 can nap.

 can nap, nap, nap, nap.

I am Dan.

I can nap with my .

We can nap, nap, nap, nap.

can nap.

 can nap, nap, nap, nap.

I am Pat.

I can nap with my .

We can nap, nap, nap, nap.

Tap with Me

by Cara Blanco

illustrated by Holli Conger

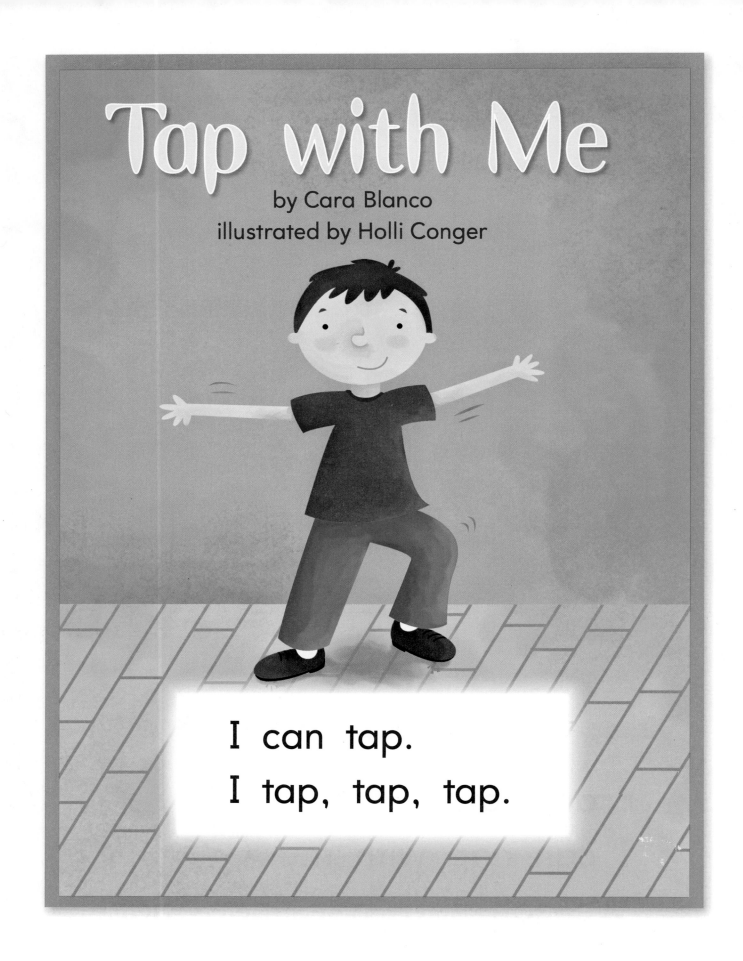

I can tap.

I tap, tap, tap.

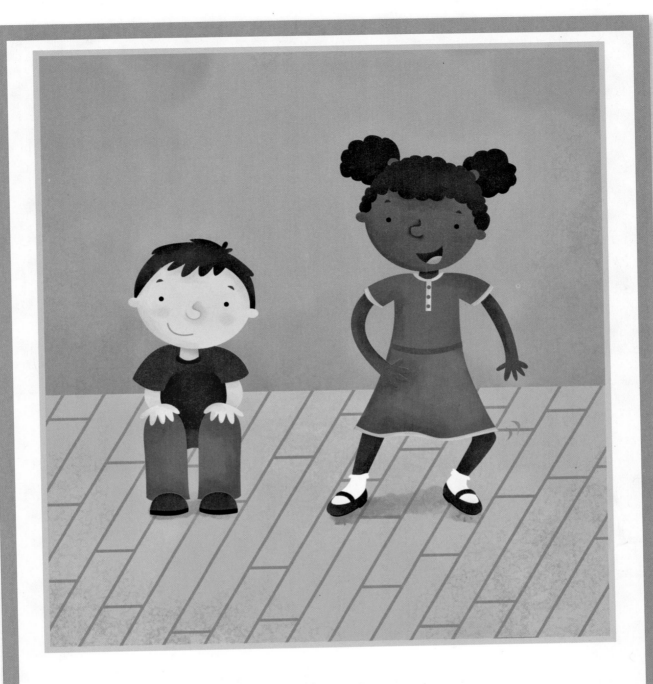

I can tap. Nan can tap.
Nan can tap, tap, tap.

I can tap with Nan.
Tap, tap, tap.

I am Tap Man!
Tap, tap, tap! Tap Man!

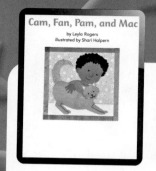

Cam, Fan, Pam, and Mac
by Leyla Rogers
illustrated by Shari Halpern

Fat Cat
by Amy Miller
illustrated by Hideko Takahashi

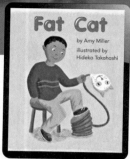

WORDS TO KNOW
High-Frequency Words

you
what

Vocabulary Reader

Context Cards

Lots of Birds

Do you see the butterfly?

How Do I Use It?
You are my best friend. Where are you going?

Talk It Over:
Take turns with a partner. Say these sentences about each other.
• You are _____ years old.
• You have _____ hair.
• You are wearing _____ socks.

Words to Know

Read Together

▸ Read the words.

▸ Talk about the pictures.

you

1

Do **you** see the butterfly?

what

2

What colors do you see?

Your Turn

Talk About It!

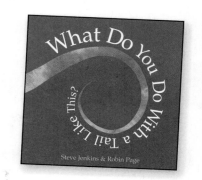

What Do You Do With a Tail Like This?

Steve Jenkins & Robin Page

How do animals use their body parts? Talk to a partner about it.

Cam, Fan, Pam, and Mac

by Leyla Rogers

illustrated by Shari Halpern

Cam can see a tan cat.

Cam can pat the tan cat.

The fat tan cat can see Cam.

Fan can see Nat.
Can Nat see Fan?
Nat can!   Nat can!

Pam can see Sam.
Sam can nap, nap, nap!
Pam sat with Sam.

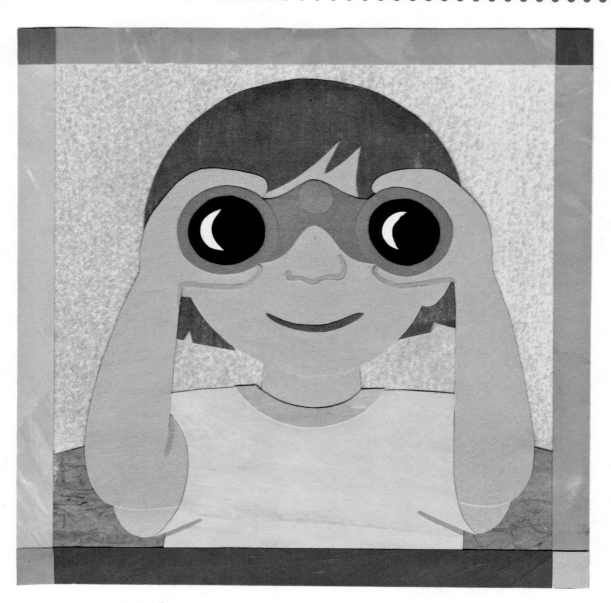

What can Mac see?
Mac can see you.

Fat Cat

by Amy Miller

illustrated by
Hideko Takahashi

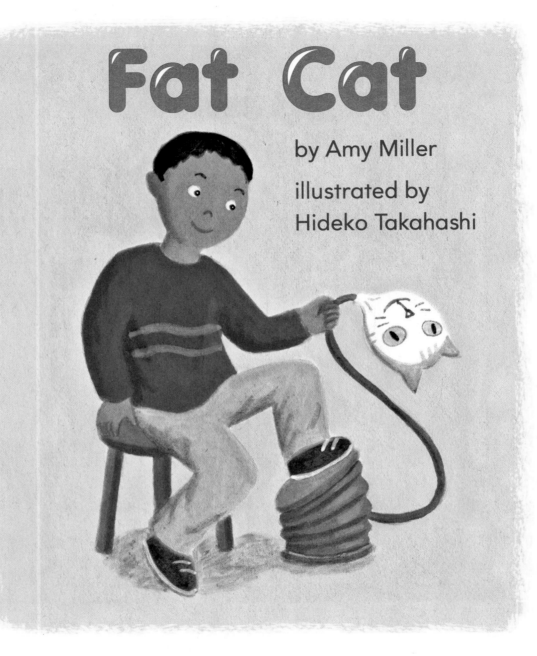

Sam sat.

Sam sat to tap, tap, tap.

Can you see the cat?
Sam can tap, tap, tap, tap.

Tap, Sam! Tap, Sam!
Tap. Tap. Tap.

Can you see the fat cat?
What a fat, fat cat!

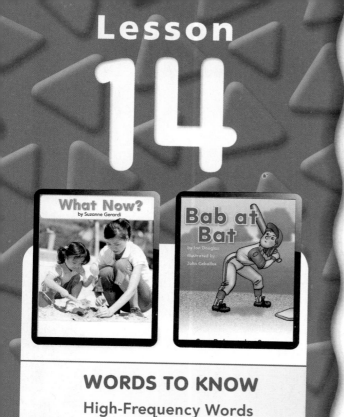

WORDS TO KNOW
High-Frequency Words

are

now

Vocabulary
Reader

Context
Cards

Words to Know

Read
Together

▶ Read the words.

▶ Talk about the pictures.

are

The turtles **are** swimming.

now

The turtle is sleeping **now**.

Your Turn

Talk About It!

What animals can you find near a pond? Talk to a partner about it.

139

What Now?
by Suzanne Gerardi

Can Pam and Nan pat?

Nan can pat now.

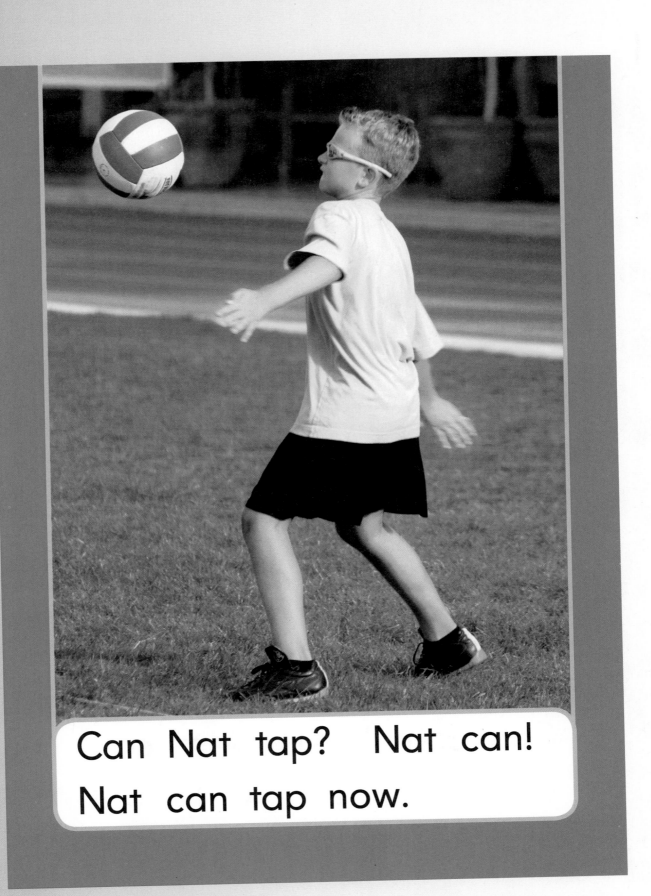

Can Nat tap? Nat can!
Nat can tap now.

Sam and Bab are at bat.
Can Sam bat? Sam can.
Bat, Sam, bat!

Now we can nap.

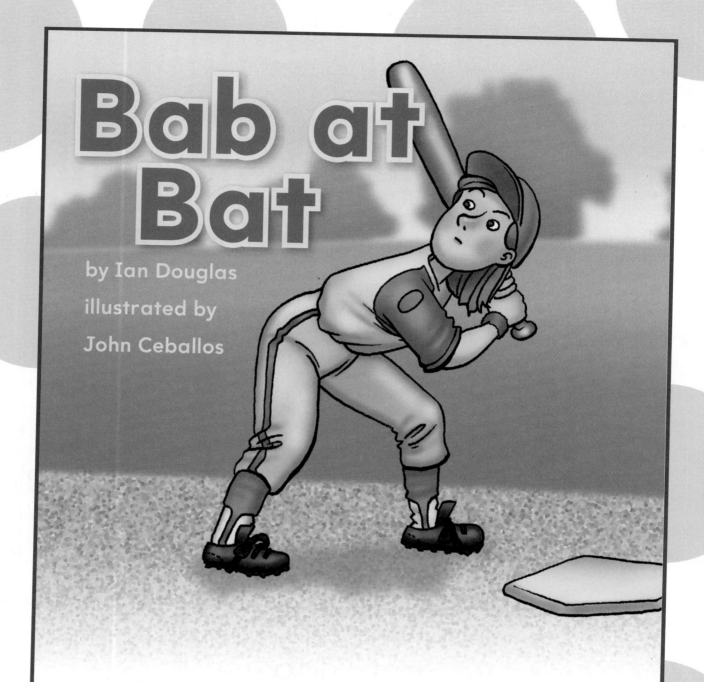

Bab at Bat

by Ian Douglas

illustrated by

John Ceballos

See Bab at bat?
Bab can bat.

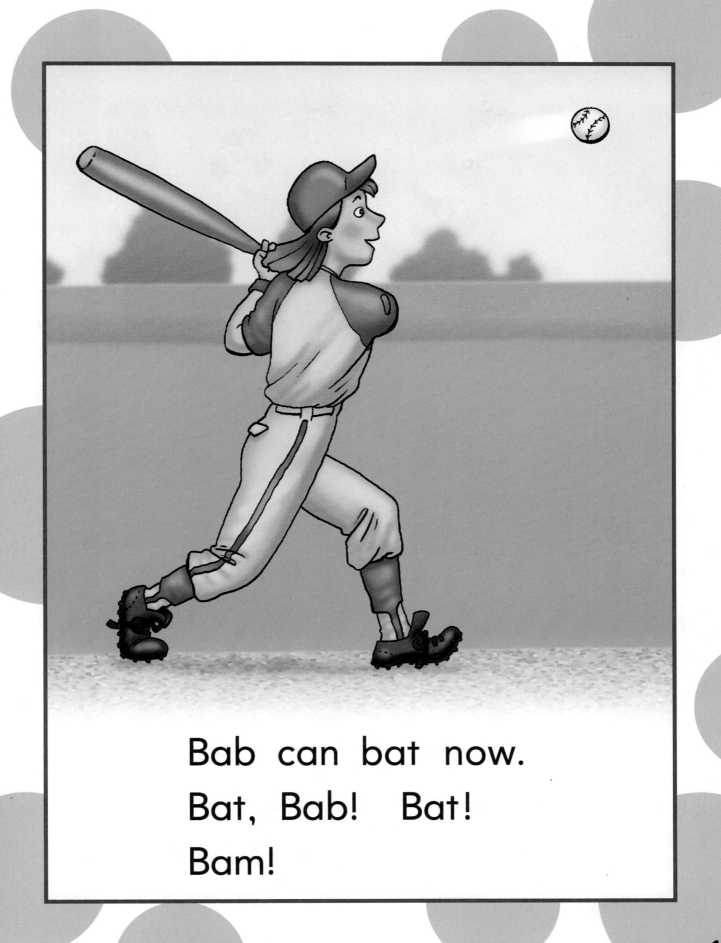

Bab can bat now.
Bat, Bab!   Bat!
Bam!

Bab CAN bat!
Pat can see Bab bat.
You can, Pat! You can!

Pat can. We can.
We are , Pat!

WORDS TO KNOW

High-Frequency Words

come

me

Vocabulary Reader

Context Cards

Words to Know

▶ You learned these words. Use each one in a sentence.

come

The rain will **come** down in spring.

me

This hat is for **me**.

Your Turn

Talk About It!

What can we see in the sky? Talk to a friend about it.

Mac and Pam Cat

by Nina Dimopolous
illustrated by Bari Weissmann

Mac sat and sat.

Pam Cat sat.
Mac can pat Pam Cat.

Mac sat with Pam Cat.
Mac can fan Pam Cat.

Come to me, Pam Cat.
Pam Cat! Pam Cat!

Come with Me

by Roger DiPaulo

illustrated by Fahimeh Amiri

Nat sat and sat.
Nat sat, sat, sat.

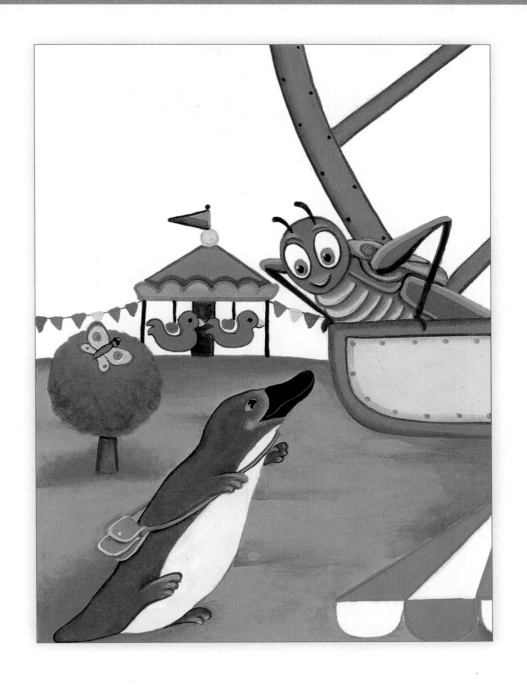

Come with me, Bab!
Bab! Bab! Bab!

Nat sat. Bab sat.
Nat can see Nan.
Bab can see Nan.

Nat sat. Bab sat. Nan sat.

Word Lists

Unit 1

Lesson

1

See What We Can Do	We Can Make It
Wordless Story	Wordless Story

Lesson

2

We Go to School	I Like
Wordless Story	**High-Frequency Words** **I**, like

Lesson

3

Baby Bear's Family	The Party
Wordless Story	**High-Frequency Words** **I, like,** the

Lesson

4

Mm	I Like Mm	
Suggested Words	**Suggested Words**	**High-Frequency Words**
masks, mice, mittens, moon, mountains, mouse, music	milk, moon, mouse, muffins	and, **I, like,** the

Lesson 5

Ss

Suggested Words

sailboat, sailing, sailor, sea, seal, soccer, sun, surf, surfboard

I Like Ss

Suggested Words

sailboat, sandwich, seal, soup, sun

High-Frequency Words

and, I, like, the

Unit 2

Lesson 6

Aa

Suggested Words

acrobats, alligator, anthill, ants, apple

I See

Suggested Words

ambulance, ants, apple, astronaut

High-Frequency Words

I, see, the

Lesson 7

Tt

Suggested Words

teddy bear, tracks, train, triangle, trampolines, tree, turtle, turtles

We Like Toys

Suggested Words

tiger, tools, toys, truck, twins

High-Frequency Words

I, like, the, we

Lesson 8

Cc

Suggested Words

camel, camels, cap, carrots, cars, castle, cat, cats, clouds, computer

I Can See

Suggested Words

castle, cat, caterpillar, computer

High-Frequency Words

a, I, see

● ● • ● • • ● • ● • ● • ● • ● ● ● ● ●

Lesson

9

Pp

Suggested Words

pajamas, pan, parachutes, pencils, penguins, pirouettes, pop, popcorn

I Like Animals

Suggested Words

pandas, parrots, pigs, polar bears

High-Frequency Words

I, like, see, to

Lesson

10

Mmmm, Good!

Suggested Words

apples, carrots, pumpkins, tomatoes

High-Frequency Words

I, like, see, to, we

The Playground

Suggested Words

jump rope, slide, sprinkler, swings, water fountain

High-Frequency Words

I, like, see, the, to, we

Unit 3 ● ● • ● • • ● • ● • ● • ● • ● ● ● ● ●

Lesson

11

Pat Cat, Sam Cat

Decodable Words

Target Skill: Words with Short *a*

am*, cat, Pat, Sam, sat

High-Frequency Words

come, I, me, to

Pam Cat

Decodable Words

Target Skill: Words with Short *a*

cat, Pam, pat, sat

High-Frequency Words

and, come, I, me, see, to

Lesson

12

I Can Nap

Decodable Words

Target Skill: Words with *n*

am*, can*, Dan, nap, Pat

High-Frequency Words

I, my, with, we

Tap with Me

Decodable Words

Target Skill: Words with *n*

am*, can*, man*, Nan, tap

High-Frequency Words

I, me, with

160

Lesson

13

Cam, Fan, Pam, and Mac

Decodable Words

Target Skill: Words with *f*

Cam, can*, cat, fan, fat, Mac, nap, Nat, Pam, pat, Sam, sat, tan

High-Frequency Words

a, and, see, what, with, you

Fat Cat

Decodable Words

Target Skill: Words with *f*

can*, cat, fat, Sam, sat, tap

High-Frequency Words

a, see, the, to, what, you

Lesson

14

What Now?

Decodable Words

Target Skill: Words with *b*

at*, Bab, bat, can*, Nan, nap, Nat, Pam, pat, Sam, tap

High-Frequency Words

and, are, now, we, what

Bab at Bat

Decodable Words

Target Skill: Words with *b*

at*, Bab, bam, bat, can*, Pat

High-Frequency Words

are, now, see, we, you

Lesson

15

Mac and Pam Cat

Decodable Words

Review Short *a, n, f, b*

can*, cat, fan, Mac, Pam, pat, sat

High-Frequency Words

and, come, me, to, with

Come with Me

Decodable Words

Review Short *a, n, f, b*

Bab, can*, Nan, Nat, sat

High-Frequency Words

and, come, me, see, with

Photo Credits

Placement Key: (r) right, (l) left, (c) center, (t) top, (b) bottom, (bg) background